SUCCESS DISMISSED

by
Personal Stories

MARYAM GOLCHOOBIAN

For inquiries or permission requests, please contact:
info@redefinebyastory.com

Print ISBN: 979-8-9904997-0-6
E-Book ISBN: 979-8-9904997-1-3
Printed in the United States

To the Unyielding Spirit of Everyday People,
May your narrative rise above the noise, reminding the world that every so-called Nobody is truly Somebody.

Acknowledgments

I am grateful for the inspiration I have received from various authors and leaders whose work has greatly influenced my own perspective. It is challenging to mention everyone, and it would be unfair to highlight some names and exclude others.

I feel privileged to have had the chance to modestly engage with their abundant sources of wisdom and insight.

Maryam Golchoobian

Contents

Dear Reader,

Welcome to this book, where authentic stories are given an opportunity to be heard, written-in-stone success concepts are challenged, and intimidating territories of entitlement are explored.

CHAPTER 1
Stories That No One Should Care About

ONCE UPON A RIGHT TIME, there was a town where everything was just so right and according to plan that anything outside the norm was neither acknowledged nor allowed to exist.

The town held the belief that everything should strive to reach its "Full Potential". It was a predetermined standard that most residents had already achieved. Among them were Mr. Powerful, Mr. Skillful, Mrs. Tactful, and Ms. Resourceful, who had all earned their "-ful" badges that symbolized their worthy achievements.

In this town, there was a middle-aged woman named Hope. She had reached her full potential in embodying hopefulness and earned her badge from the town mayor as Ms. Hopeful.

Despite this, she struggled to gain the respect and acceptance of the townsfolk. They constantly questioned why she was not contributing in more practical and meaningful ways.

The residents also doubted individuals like Mr. Painful, whose unpleasant behavior caused others pain, yet that pain was seen as necessary for personal growth and achievement.

Likewise, there was Mr. Wonderful, whose glamorous nature made people question his contributions beyond mere distractions and self-promotion.

However, he quickly cleared away those doubts by showing how his presence attracted investment opportunities to the town's properties and promoted the local tourism industry. After all, who wouldn't be tempted to invest in a town filled with wonderful opportunities?

So, in a community where everyone focused on tangible outcomes, offering hope when it wasn't truly needed, resulted in others ignoring Hope's contributions. Every time she took part in important meetings and gatherings, she felt isolated and excluded.

She was denied the chance to speak up and share her thoughts because others believed she was out of touch with reality. They primarily valued tangible things, unlike her idealistic beliefs in the power of hope.

One day, the residents, tired of Hope's empty gestures and what they saw as hollow promises, gathered for a meeting with the town's senior members, including Mr. Powerful, who held considerable influence over town affairs. Nearly everyone in that meeting voted in favor of permanently expelling Hope from the town.

So, on a freezing December morning, when everyone was enjoying the warmth of their cozy homes and celebrating the holiday, Ms. Hopeful gathered her belongings and left the town, tears pouring down her face. However, she held onto her strong hope that one day, she would return to the town where her presence was truly valued and appreciated.

With each passing day, the residents not only did not regret Hope's departure, but whenever they crossed paths, they nodded in approval, affirming the rightness of their decision to rid the town of what they believed was a burden. They felt a sense of relief to be free from her impassioned yet empty speeches about hope and dreams.

Over the years, those who prioritized measurable outcomes intensified their efforts, doubling down on hard work, and transformed the town into a remarkable and influential one.

After several Successful years, on a foggy October day, when everything seemed perfect in the town, something happened that disrupted the perfect routine.

It started at Mr. Powerful's home, but before long, most of the people in the town became trapped in its web. It resembled a serious epidemic or a completely unknown illness that puzzled the scientific community. The reason and solution for the condition appeared to be a mystery and all the efforts to fully understand it were useless.

As time went on, more and more people experienced hollowed eyes, weakened bodies, and an endless thirst. They asked Ms. Resourceful for help, but she admitted that she lacked the answers when it came to unsolved scientific problems.

Although she occasionally managed to cure rare cancer cases, such as Mr. Mindful's, with the help of specific treatment plans and firm discipline, when faced with a widespread outbreak affecting individuals of typical potential and ability, she was incapable of intervening.

They gathered the most knowledgeable and skillful experts in the field of science, and after months of research, instead of giving a clear answer, they admitted that they couldn't find a solution. They simply said, "All that's left is hope."

"But hope?" Mr. Powerful objected. "That's absurd! We've already expelled hope from the town, and we haven't even bothered to keep track of her whereabouts."

After holding several public and private meetings, finally with Mr. Helpful's assistance, they formed teams of citizens to search for Hope. Each group was eventually replaced by a new one after weeks of dedicated search, and still, no one could locate her.

The situation became extremely serious, and Mr. Powerful issued a firm ultimatum: unless they became fully resourceful in finding a way to locate Hope, he would sell off all his possessions, withdraw his investments from the stock market, and set off on a journey with his son to distant lands in search of a cure.

As the fear for their lives grew, people rallied together, putting in their best efforts. They formed spy teams and used the services of private investigators to search every town across the country in hopes of finding Hope.

With each passing day, as the chances of locating her decreased, a private detective, Mr. Insightful, worn out from his door-to-door investigations in a small town, found himself taking a break near a bush close to a jungle.

While he was relaxing and at the same time strategically planning his next steps, he witnessed something unusual: a woman carrying a lamp even though it was daylight, and she also had a food basket with her, heading towards the jungle.

Mr. Insightful, who had a reputation for his sharp observations, found it strange for someone to be involved in such unproductive actions during the day.

Intrigued by this scene, he chose to follow the woman into the jungle. He observed as she set down the lamp and food basket, and then carried on with pouring oil into the lamp. The lamp produced a thick but bright smoky cloud that rose high into the sky, much like the magic lamps of old tales.

The woman had covered her face with a shawl to protect herself from the cold weather, making it impossible for the detective to determine if she was Hope.

Even if her face was visible, it had been more than ten years since her expulsion from the town. The difficulties she faced during that time could have greatly changed her appearance and made it hard to recognize her right away.

Deciding to follow the woman to her residence, Mr. Insightful was confident that eventually she would reveal her face, or he would at least know her place. As they approached her modest dwelling, darkness fell, but the candles outside her home were already lit.

Instead of going straight to her home, the woman sat on a wooden table near a stream, trying to clean the mud off her boots. While doing so, she took off her shawl, exposing a face full of wrinkles and her snowy white hair.

Mr. Insightful realized that it was impossible for Hope to have aged so drastically in just ten years. As the detective approached the woman, he couldn't help but see the clear signs of deep sadness written on her face. Deep lines grooved her forehead and crossed her entire face.

Coming from the Right town, where time management was highly valued and every moment mattered, Mr. Insightful was fixed on his task. He fully recognized the need to stay focused and did not waste any time on unrelated matters. So, he immediately questioned her about any signs of Ms. Hope nearby.

The woman seemed willing to help but said she didn't recognize anyone by that name and insisted that she couldn't help without more information or clarifications. But when the detective presented her with a picture, she broke down in tears when she saw that.

She started talking nonstop about the ways in which Hope had helped her in the past and continued to do so. She also mentioned that she had nothing and no one to rely on but Hope.

The detective paused briefly, unsure if the woman's response was due to forgetfulness or confusion. He even doubted whether she might be fabricating a story because of her mental state.

Considering that Hope was known for offering encouragement and support mainly through words, the detective struggled to understand how she considered Hope's actions useful in any way.

As he continued talking to the woman, she began to share her own deeply devastating story. She told him about the time when she lost her seven-year-old son in the jungle while they were gathering firewood.

Her son had innocently wandered away from her, and no matter how desperately she called out and searched, he remained out of reach. She went back home with nothing but emptiness and overwhelmed by never-ending sadness. Her despair became more overwhelming as the days passed and her son seemed to have vanished into thin air.

In her darkest moments, she made up her mind to put an end to her suffering once and for all. She was in the middle of her distressing plan and on the edge of making her final move, just one step away from the wooden chair...

But she found herself immobilized, as if someone had a firm hold on her feet. When she opened her eyes, she saw Hope holding tightly onto her feet with tears running down her face as she mourned her own sorrows—being cast out from her roots, her hometown.

While Hope was determined to disrupt the woman's tragic plan, she yelled and begged for Hope to free her. "Don't you see?" she cried out desperately.

"I just want it all to end. I've lost everything, and I simply want to find peace..."

Hope, who had never felt so short of hope, asked the woman: "Please, give me one reason... only one... to make me believe that all hope is lost, and then I will let you go..."

In that very challenging moment, the woman shared her heartbreaking story in detail. But Hope insisted that unless she could offer proof of her son's death, a faint spark of hope survived. So, the woman's reason was not convincing enough for Hope to let go of her hold. The woman tried many times, but it seemed in vain. She was exhausted and about to collapse. Just in time, Hope promptly removed the rope off her neck.

From that moment on, Hope began visiting the woman every evening upon her return from the jungle. Not only did Hope share inspiring stories, but she also assisted the woman to apply them into her daily routines.

She motivated her to craft around twenty wooden signs each day and hang them from tree branches along her way home. These signs would help lost individuals in finding their way back to the town. Every day, Hope guided the woman along a different path, exploring new paths to increase the likelihood of lost people finding their way home.

Whether those signs were helpful for the woman's missing son or another person in need, Hope remained optimistic that there was still a chance for everyone to notice the signs and find their way. After all, in such a massive jungle, anyone was prone to getting lost, but not everyone had the resources to navigate their way back without the help of the signs.

The detective was impressed by Hope's commitment and dedication to the woman and praised her for it. It was the first time someone from the Right community had acknowledged Hope in such a way.

As Hope returned to her hometown, the townspeople greeted her with joy, cheering and shouting as they saw her approaching. She was filled with enthusiasm for being allowed to enter the Right town once more and she began spreading hope like never before.

So, discouraging comments such as "I don't think so" and "It is in vain" soon transformed into expressions like "I hope so" and "As long as there's life, there's hope."

With this resilient mindset, everyone put in more effort, spending extra time on research, taking better care of their health, and maintaining cleaner eating habits.

Before long, a vaccine for the deadly virus was discovered. The residents named it "Hope4XYZ," ensuring that no matter the nature of the excuse virus, there would never be a single case where Hope wasn't needed...

I hope you enjoyed the "Hope" story! If so, let's move on to the second story, which is a real one... However, I should warn you that this is a story, according to "The Success Rules," you should pay no attention to. But if we don't explore such stories, how can we dismiss success?!

A "Not Yet Story" Is a "Nothing Story"!

Life soon taught me that there are stars, and then there are dark stars and denying this obvious convention was no easy task.

I was the one with the dim light right from the start. Social situations made me feel awkward, and navigating the intricacies of effective communication was a huge challenge. As a result, I often retreated into my own thoughts and preferred solitary reflection over being a part of almost any group.

As I grew older, things took a turn for the worse. Despite numerous attempts to have meaningful connections with my peers, I only crossed paths with a handful of like-minded individuals.

However, I never fully embraced this way of life. It felt like swallowing ice cubes, one after another. I highly doubt anyone could master this skill!

Every effort to escape or seek help quickly proved to be a hidden trap. Eventually, I surrendered my attempts to better my own life and yielded to the illusion that it was all over and convinced myself to prioritize improving the lives of others instead.

Although selflessly dedicating my time and resources to others around me and engaging in some volunteer activities brought some joy and a sense of purpose to my life, they say "If you have one choice, you have no choice."

I still felt too young to give up on a more meaningful life, especially when I witnessed everyone around me seemingly were on their own personal journeys.

I tried different things, including being obsessively engaged in hobbies like reading and painting, but it felt as if I wasn't just jumping between branches, but swinging through the trees!

Apart from holding a part-time, low-wage teaching job consistently, I found it challenging to maintain a stable career. The curse of my impaired social skills always hindered my progress and prevented me from staying on a single path long enough to see any meaningful outcomes.

Once I thought that perhaps the reason, I persisted to do something meaningful with my life was because I lived in a busy capital city, surrounded by people leading hectic lives, and I yearned for a similar existence.

I believed that relocating to a quieter place and engaging in more solitary activities that brought me joy would make things more tolerable. Yet, moving to a smaller city for a few months did not resolve anything, and I found myself unable to escape the constant sense of dissatisfaction and inner unrest.

Years went by in a similar manner, with no clear answers to the many questions swirling in my mind about why I always felt uncomfortable and different. Several therapy and counseling sessions also did not work for me.

One day, after watching a British movie that I had seen more than a hundred times that year because of its beautiful sceneries and compelling story plot, a voice whispered in my ear and urged me to start a journey to unknown experiences to reach a completely different emotional state.

So, I thought, why not consider this new experience at my favorite university in the world? I had always admired Newcastle University with its dark red bricks, mesmerizing architecture, and atmosphere.

So, within just a few quick months of feeling that strong urge, I found myself at Newcastle airport, ready to start a journey filled with all sorts of magical experiences right from the start.

While I committed myself to excelling in that postgraduate course, I also took my time exploring beautiful castles, abbeys, and historic sites, trying to make the most of every minute of it.

As I neared the end of my time there, I couldn't shake the feeling that the enchantment would soon fade away. I worried that once again I would be consumed by a sense of emptiness and lack of direction, the same despair that had brought me to that place.

Like many people worldwide, registering for the US Visa Lottery had become a yearly habit for me, and sometimes I even forgot to check the results. However, that particular year was very different because I strongly hesitated to go back home and continuously searched for my next chance to escape.

On yet another misty and gloomy morning, as I scrolled through my emails searching for some notifications, I suddenly remembered that it was time to check the Visa Lottery results. I couldn't recall a time in my life when I needed something as desperately as winning that lottery.

To my amazement, I discovered that I had won! I won something that was seen by many as a green ticket to a land of new opportunities, a place for those who never even had their first one. Trying to hold back that level of excitement was pointless, and my loud shouts of joy in the early morning ended up causing me some trouble later!

So, in less than a year, I arrived at LAX, eagerly waiting for a family friend to pick me up. I thought I was about to start a totally unique and exciting adventure. However, from the beginning, it was nothing like I had imagined.

Just within a couple of months and after a few disagreements with my flat mate, mainly because of my introverted routines, I had to find my own place and live independently. It quickly became clear that this would be the most challenging journey of my life.

Many Americans are familiar with the difficulties of building credit. As a foreigner with no credit history, securing a decent rental deal, or any deal for that matter, can be incredibly difficult, if not impossible. So, after much effort, I managed to pay a high deposit fee and rent an apartment in an unsafe neighborhood in LA called K-Town. Not only was the neighborhood known for its dangers, but the building I rented a suite in had its own set of issues.

The place was filled with people, many of whom spoke very limited English and presence of numerous red flags such as frequent altercations made me concerned about their potential criminal background. To feel safe, I purchased various self-defense tools like pepper spray and a stun gun. But I struggled to use them effectively and quickly during several potentially dangerous situations, so they did not make me feel safe enough.

Another significant issue for me was the frequent intrusion of strong weed smoke into my apartment. It was a real problem since I am prone to allergies, and this resulted in persistent rashes and some respiratory discomfort.

My next-door neighbor, a man in his late forties or early fifties, lived with his even more unstable girlfriend. Their disruptive behavior went beyond what could be only due to their weed use.

Neither of them seemed to have a job, and they spent most of their time at home, engaging in loud and violent fights almost every day. Their arguments would frequently escalate to a point where the LAPD had to intervene, regardless of the time, day, or night.

Their shouts of “Open the door, LAPD!” often abruptly woke me up from my already nightmarish sleep. It wasn’t just their voices; it was the resounding thuds of their boots pounding against that neighbor’s door. The vibrations were so intense that I feared the century-old windows in my apartment would shatter at any moment.

The couple often engaged in such heated arguments that they refused to open the door for a good fifteen minutes.

As a result, I witnessed a scene straight out of a Hollywood movie, with the police diligently working to gain entry. Given my heightened sensory sensitivity, nothing proved more torturous in that process than the sound of police helicopters circling for extended periods over the building.

While that couple were not the sole source of trouble in that three-story apartment complex, it certainly seemed like they commanded most of the LAPD's attention.

All of this was totally new to me. In my hometown abroad, where I lived by myself in a pleasant neighborhood, I had never experienced such visible chaos or felt so unsafe at home.

While Los Angeles is a beautiful city with numerous great places and nice neighborhoods, my narrative focused on the place where I could afford to live and the challenges it presented, especially for a foreigner living alone.

When it came to career and employment, I had already lost hope in things improving and felt inadequate even before I arrived in the US. Even though I tried to divert my attention from such feelings through different methods, the fact that I did not make a living on my own always made me feel down.

My academic degrees were either outdated or irrelevant in the United States, which made them seem worthless. Moreover, because I was unfamiliar with the norms, I viewed certain jobs as unacceptable or inappropriate. I had no idea that was the same path most immigrants or even residents in a similar situation were supposed to take.

As a result, I persisted and concentrated on finding any kind of job in an office environment, rather than working in malls, restaurants, or warehouses. So, I managed to avoid taking on any employment for about a year while attending college. I was trying to find a quick solution that would secure me a decent office job.

To make a long story short, after facing multiple disappointments and rejections, I eventually obtained a position related to that major in a reputable medical center.

While working there, I faced ongoing mistreatment and outright bullying from most of my coworkers who considered me as a naive and boring person. Despite this, I persevered and excelled in that position. I even received some recognition that seemed to overshadow their years of experience, which only made them treat me with more unkindness.

These daily challenges and disappointments did not stop me from devoting significant time and effort to obtain some managerial-level certifications in that field.

Typically, it takes individuals several years to accumulate enough experience and knowledge necessary to successfully pass those tests. However, by earning the highest-level credential in that field much sooner, I was able to increase my initial salary to more than double that amount within a couple of years.

Even though I gave it my all in my job, I never saw it as my true calling in life. I had heard about various money-making opportunities in the US, so I started exploring and learning as much as I could. I began watching YouTube videos, reading relevant contents, and staying updated to the best of my ability, all with the hope of finding opportunities that could improve my situation and allow me to leave the corporate world.

While exploring such opportunities, I created a website from scratch to try affiliate marketing and signed up to join multiple websites and paid subscriptions related to angel investing and trading back in 2018.

By taking their lead, I invested in a diverse range of startups and explored some other side hustle and investing opportunities, but unfortunately, none of them have yielded the desired outcome so far.

Not being part of any 5 AM club, I found myself waking up even earlier out of necessity. Balancing the mental fatigue from my demanding full-time corporate job was already a challenge, but the truly overwhelming part was navigating through social difficulties and enduring constant bullying.

My social life was minimal, and I only had a couple of friends who were also caught up in their own busy lives. I could only count on them in emergencies.

Some years before, a doctor suggested that I might have a condition known as Asperger's, which is a former term used to describe individuals on the high-functioning end of the autism spectrum.

I never felt a strong urge to pursue a formal diagnosis until I reached around the age of 40. However, as I continued to research the condition more, I discovered that it provided answers to many of the questions I had. But unfortunately, these newfound insights did not necessarily make my journey any easier to bear.

I recall a time when I shared this information with the management at one of my workplaces, hoping it would help resolve some misunderstandings. Regrettably, it turned out to be the biggest mistake I could have made.

Despite my almost perfect professional performance, that ultimately led to my resignation as a means to prevent facing literal termination from the job.

Meanwhile, I frequently found myself being regarded as a potential threat in the workplace, whether it was due to occasional acts of insubordination by voicing my opinions or being seen as overqualified.

This placed me in a frustrating cycle of securing promising positions, only to leave them before making any progress or receiving any substantial promotion, depleting my savings between jobs with long orientations.

So, my strategy for handling money was to save as much as I could for the never-ending rainy days. It might seem a bit extreme, but I didn't even make a single trip back home or take any vacations during my entire seven-year stay in the United States.

I made the choice to prioritize saving, primarily due to constant fear of job insecurity and the high possibility of needing to enter survival mode at any given moment.

One day, after almost depleting all my funds during a job transition, I found myself with just a few thousand dollars in credit. Unfortunately, when I received an eviction notice, the building management insisted on accepting only payment in the form of a check or cash.

To timely cover that month's rent, I had to sell some personal items and quickly get rid of the rest so to vacate the flat within the specified 30-day notice period and return home.

Meanwhile, I continued to apply for various jobs, eagerly hoping for any opportunity that would come my way. I soon received a response from a department store in downtown LA, inviting me for an interview.

Given my limited social skills and the expectation to excel in these skills as a sales associate, I really doubted about my chances of landing the job. However, I was fortunate enough to meet a compassionate Egyptian woman who conducted the interview. Her empathy and understanding made the process much easier for me, allowing me to secure enough funds for the next month's rent.

Under normal circumstances, people typically lean on their close friends and family for support during challenging times. However, I was determined to keep my struggles hidden, and my close friends were not intimate enough for me to discuss such matters with them.

While working at that department store, I continued to actively apply for corporate positions, and soon, I obtained one in a relatively large company in downtown LA.

In the following years of my stay in the United States, despite achieving some recognition from the management in my corporate roles across different companies and possessing the necessary certifications and experience to even secure some managerial level positions in that field, I was trapped in a toxic cycle that I mentioned earlier.

I faced consequences that had nothing to do with the professional aspect of my job and ultimately, these circumstances left me with no choice but to quit my jobs one after another, especially during the last year of my stay in the United States.

In the end, I found myself in an overwhelmingly difficult situation. Surviving within that cycle seemed almost impossible. I felt sadness and exhaustion with every cell in my body and did not see any point in continuing a fight that got me nowhere but a burned-out physical and mental state.

For seven challenging years, I persevered through hardships, constantly compromising my standard of living and occasionally lived below the poverty line. In the end, I had to return home without any tangible accomplishments or results. The only intangible result was proving to myself I survived on my own for several years...

It feels like I compressed my story into an MP4 file, just giving a quick glimpse of a journey that seemed to lack a clear destination—a journey with a "Not Yet" Destination.

Do I believe that my story is unique or distinct compared to the stories of other immigrants or individuals facing harsh conditions? Not truly. Many people, have endured tremendously challenging situations, even reaching the point of literal homelessness, and yet their stories are often overlooked.

That is because the focus was never intended to be mainly on the stories themselves, as the saying goes:

"No one cares about your story UNTIL you win, so win..."

I was unaware of the origin of this quote, but after some research, it seems that accurately tracing its source is difficult. While variations of this statement or mindset have been expressed by multiple individuals mainly in the personal growth and coaching field, the specific origin of this quote appears to be unknown.

The primary objective of this book is not to focus on specific individuals or engage in criticism of the entire industry. Rather, the intention is to reflect on my observations regarding the widespread presence of such quotes and mindsets in social media contents.

These observations may help increase awareness and sensitivity to these subjects among experts in various fields, inspiring them to pay greater attention to such areas and trends.

Let's examine this quote and the similar statements that have been circulating on social media. It's all about personal stories and how they are perceived.

When it comes to sports competitions, it's evident that not everyone can expect attention or recognition. Nobody seems to pay attention to a person who finishes 10th in a marathon or cycling race, regardless of the reasons for their underperformance.

However, similar quotes are frequently used in everyday contexts where winning is perceived as an extraordinary, impressive, and grand accomplishment in life. It's almost as if every story is expected to center around a monumental victory, and if that is not the case it is treated as a nobody's story.

I devised the phrase "Celebritized Greatness - Unisized Success," which reflects this mindset. In essence, it suggests that achieving remarkable levels of greatness and success, by predetermined standards, is necessary to have a story considered worthy of telling.

When success is exclusively defined in terms of concrete achievements with strict standards, personal stories and lives that diverge from this norm are often easily dismissed as insignificant and unworthy of attention.

So, this mindset often fails to appreciate the depth and intricacy of everyday human experiences by underestimating the importance of the journey itself.

It implies that nobody cares about your life experiences because the concluding part of your story didn't meet our standards, or maybe not yet. I would like to refer to this perspective as "The End of the Story Elusion," which can be more discouraging rather than motivating.

This mindset often eclipses the meaningful journeys of self-improvement and incremental achievements which can ultimately create a paradox in personal growth and self-improvement contents. The emphasis on "winning" tends to overshadow or entirely neglect the significance of failure, adversity, and their valuable lessons that are essential for personal development.

Should we consider that non-winning stories can also provide meaningful insights? Or does the depth and worth of personal stories rely exclusively on their outcome? And, most importantly, how much importance should we place on other people's "Care" compared to the message itself, when we decide to share our stories?

Have those who advocate such quotes adequately explained the reasons why others should care about our stories in the first place? Do they imply that people should care so that we can potentially gain something from being heard? Or do they suggest that if others don't care, these stories have a low chance of being transformed into amazing episodes, movies, or books?

On the contrary, should the main motive for sharing our stories be more genuine, such as inspiring, educating, or uplifting by their authentic human experiences, rather than their standardized outcomes?

Some people may argue that personal stories lack intrinsic value and are only used as attention-grabbing accessories to gain personal benefits. They may propose that personal stories should be treated as luxurious items that not everyone can afford to have one. However, should it truly be that way?

These questions prompt us to consider how we use, or should use, our personal stories. Are they meant to serve as practical tools or are they mere accessories?

Within the context of everyday life, it seems we have been sharing these stories for numerous purposes. People frequently share their stories in support groups, community events or just in social gatherings. These stories may be utilized in job applications and interviews as examples or evidence to support qualifications. People also tell these stories to their children to instill values and life lessons or just to communicate standards and expectations.

A relatable example to show the negative impact of such a one-sided mindset is when parents share their stories, and achievements with their children and their stories are compared to these "winning stories".

This comparison can lead younger generations to exhibit disrespect and disobedience. Under the influence of these motivational quotes, some children may silently question their parents, "Are you even qualified to offer advice? You don't fit their definition of a 'Winner'..."

The same scenario applies to schoolteachers and all individuals who may need to rely on storytelling more regularly to shape the minds and souls of the young individuals under their care and education.

So, it seems that personal stories are more than mere decorative items reserved for special occasions. They can be acknowledged as powerful tools for education, connection, empathy, and understanding, among others, irrespective of how they conclude.

When we share our authentic experiences and perspectives, we contribute to a deeper and more significant collective consciousness.

Now someone might question, what the main motive could be behind suppressing and discouraging individuals from sharing their stories in this way, or perhaps preventing them from daring to share their stories with a broader or global audience?

Do these leaders suggest that it is not the "Right Time" to share these stories because they have not yet reached a victorious conclusion?

If the answer to the above question is yes, then most likely, they have used "Celebritized Greatness-Unisized Success" as a filter for our personal stories. This concept acts as a barrier for numerous narratives and as a result only the most prominent stories, those that closely resemble their own, endure. This may result in the subtle monopolization of Greatness and Success over time.

However, if everyday people's stories were to suggest that Greatness and Success can be evaluated using different criteria, rather than solely being fixated on the end of the story, they have the potential to redirect attention away from current trends.

These prevailing trends on social media, saturated with such quotes and contents, that redirect attention from the "story" to the "storyteller," make every minor challenge encountered by some public figures elicit significantly more emotional reactions and attention than the deeply impactful experiences of ordinary individuals.

Developing this mindset over time can lead to a distortion of our perception of justice and empathy. Individuals who face daily challenges in pursuit of their goals and dreams are frequently labeled as "losers" simply because they have not reached their desired destination.

As a result, those in positions of power may adopt this mindset to justify their lack of empathy and understanding towards the stories of these so-called average and ordinary individuals.

The stories that could otherwise greatly help them in finding suitable solutions for many existing problems with their subordinates are often overlooked. This ignorance and disregard for personal narratives, dismissing them as unworthy, can ultimately compromise the mental well-being of their employees or subordinates.

Such a perspective on their narratives prevents the everyday individuals from utilizing their stories to advocate for better treatments, promotions, or work-life balance.

To give an example, people with such a mindset may fail to recognize that success, for a young single mother without sufficient awareness or education, could involve overcoming her ongoing challenges with drinking to create a nurturing environment at home where her children can feel safer and receive the attention they deserve.

Many individuals may not have the opportunity or potential to share their stories within larger communities. However, paradoxically, it is within smaller communities and micro-societies that personal stories hold significant power and can create meaningful impacts, facilitating transformative shifts in societal culture.

Throughout history, we have witnessed numerous examples of such stories that support this point. While I have highlighted some of the historical figures in this book, there are countless others whose stories equally deserve recognition.

So, it is crucial for us, everyday individuals, to recognize the significance of our personal narratives and refrain from dismissing them as mere tales of failure.

CHAPTER 2

A Man Smarter Than Einstein

"Try not to become a man of success, but rather try to become a man of value."

–Attributed to Albert Einstein

ONCE UPON A DREAM TIME, there was a man who had a deep fascination with physics, but he never had the chance to pursue his passion in the field. He firmly believed that if given the chance, he could surpass even Einstein.

For him, physics symbolized the intricate connections between tangible things, and during his discussions he frequently used comments like "It doesn't make sense according to the laws of physics."

When asked to elaborate, he would point to Einstein's famous equation, $E=MC^2$, as an example. However, his understanding of the equation was very inaccurate. He interpreted it as; even Energy is a Compound form of Matter.

The man lacked a basic understanding of physics and used these assumptions to influence naive individuals with his tailored advice. He often encouraged others to remain grounded in reality rather than becoming lost in their thoughts.

One day, the man had a dream in which he met Einstein.

Einstein introduced himself as the godfather of physics and offered to become the man's mentor. Internally, Einstein couldn't help but feel a sense of frustration towards man's superficial understanding and misinterpretations.

The man eagerly accepted the opportunity and ready to undertake any tasks assigned by his favorite mentor.

Einstein began with a simple question: "Are you familiar with counting?" The man confidently nodded and responded that there were indeed two people in the room.

Einstein then instructed the man, saying, "When you wake up, take a piece of paper and a pen, go out wherever you want, and observe carefully."

He advised the man to draw a line on the paper and create two columns: one for things that can be counted and/or tangible ones, and another for things that can't be counted, uncountable items, and/or intangible ones. Einstein encouraged him to use "all his senses" while carrying out the task.

"Upon your return," Einstein promised, "I guarantee that you will receive everything you've listed as countable/tangible, and I will remove from your possession all the items you listed as uncountable/intangible. Can we agree on this deal?" asked Einstein.

The man was so tempted by the proposition that he didn't hesitate for a moment. After all, he had spent his entire life advising others to focus on tangible items. The opportunity to acquire all the tangible things he desired was beyond his wildest dreams.

In an instant, he envisioned himself strolling through jewelry shops, admiring luxurious cars in galleries, and exploring magnificent mansions. The mere thought fascinated him enough to strike a deal with Einstein.

Once the agreement was finalized, he woke up and immediately got to work. He wasted no time as he diligently began his task. With strong determination, he started purchasing new notebooks, making sure not to overlook any tangible item that could be counted and claimed as his own.

His fingertips developed calluses from the tireless effort, completely forgetting about the list of things that couldn't be counted.

When he eventually remembered that uncountable list, he thought about his friendships and promptly added dozens of them to the list. He believed that when he became wealthy, his current average and ordinary friends would come to him seeking benefits, which he felt would diminish his life. He decided it was better to remove them from his life sooner rather than later.

Furthermore, he rationalized that with all his magnificent possessions, kindness was no longer necessary and seemed like a weakness to possess. He recalled the cold, bold faces of some iconic figures and how their popularity and attractiveness seemed to be enhanced by their lack of kindness. He believed that not having this often-perceived sign of weakness would bring him greater prestige.

He convinced himself that as the one in charge, he no longer required anyone else's kindness. He was confident that he could simply fulfill his desires through power rather than relying on such weak strategies. As a result, he added kindness to that very list as well.

He was thinking about adding sadness and anger to the list but ultimately decided against it. He realized that there would be no point in doing so. With an abundance of blessings, he convinced himself that he would no longer experience such negative emotions.

He then included hope on the list as well, questioning its significance when he already possessed everything he hoped for. What had "hope" ever achieved for him or anyone else, except for consistently bringing disappointment throughout his life?

His confidence soared as he firmly believed that caring about the uncountable items was irrelevant and a waste of time. He felt so indifferent toward losing those items as long as he obtained all the tangible possessions he longed for.

One night, as his bedroom was nearly overflowing with notebooks, occupying half the available space, he felt it was time for the second encounter with Einstein in his dream.

As soon as he fell asleep, he found Einstein already standing there with his disheveled hair, profound gaze, and a warm, genuine smile.

The man was filled with excitement and all he desired was a confirmation that the agreement remained intact. Einstein nodded in a reassuring manner that everything was as agreed, and nothing had changed. However, he kindly asked to examine what the man had gathered and asked for the most significant notebook as a sample.

Einstein suggested, "Instead of reviewing all your notebooks while you're in a dream state, which would require you to spend an entire month sleeping, let's go over one as a sample right here. I assure you that I will read and take action based on the contents of the remaining notebooks while you're awake."

The man readily agreed and handed over the first notebook to him. Einstein skimmed through the list, muttering the contents to himself.

The list in the notebook included numerous entries, such as "Diamonds in X Diamond Shop in Y City, Z State, Diamonds in X1 Diamond Shop in Y1 City, Z1 State, Diamonds in X2 Diamond Shop in Y2 City, Z2 State," and so on. The list extended to include hundreds of Xs, Ys, and Zs because clarity was crucial to refer to each distinct tangible item.

Merely stating "diamonds" would not be sufficient. It was crucial to specify the locations of the shops, and the corresponding cities and states. This level of clarity should be applied to all tangible and valuable dreams.

As Einstein reviewed several pages, he told the man, "Alright, I have comprehended your patterns, and to be honest, they are the simplest patterns I have ever encountered. The formula of 'the more, the better' applies to all the entries. With this straightforward formula, I will possess all the answers, and I guarantee that you will obtain all these desired possessions. However, regarding the intangible items, please guide me to the room where we can find those notebooks."

The man's initial smile vanished, replaced by nearly bursting laughter. "Which room?" he replied with disbelief. "Are you kidding, Sir? There's no room for things that can't even be counted. I didn't even bother wasting my money on a notebook to write them down."

He continued, "I just used the empty margins of this newspaper to write down the intangible items and that is all I bothered to note."

Einstein gazed at him with a mischievous twinkle in his eye, a sparkle only the godfather of Physics could possess. "So, I hope you haven't forgotten about our deal, the requirement of a minimum of 10 separate items in each list" he said playfully.

The man simply replied, "Do as you wish." Einstein then reached for the pencil tucked behind his ear and began to write. "The first item," he said aloud, "is your True Self. The one that resides within..."

"I mean your inner self. It's different from identity and personality. I aim to take away your 'I'. Well, I don't expect you to fully grasp this concept. You will only understand it through experience, and I am unsure if you have ever truly felt its presence before."

In his mind, the man couldn't help but think, "Oh, come on, father! Enough with the lecture. I'm tired of empty words. Just give me those XYZ keys before I open my eyes."

However, he knew he had to maintain a polite and patient manner to reach his dreams. So, he pretended he understood that and replied, "Oh, Sir, that is perfectly fine. I can still enjoy my dreams. It doesn't matter if Mr. X within me enjoys it, or Mr. Y, or Mr. Z. As long as I have this physical body, that's absolutely fine... I can still see the same person in the mirror, and that is more than enough."

As Einstein proceeded to mention the next item, "Inner Peace," the man made a bitter confession: "Sir, I never had it to begin with, and I'm perfectly content with that because I know why I lacked it, and I am sure I will gain it soon."

In fact, the man couldn't help but wonder if his physicist mentor had recently attended some fancy classes on positive thinking or yoga that were not available decades ago. It amused him to think how opinionated and detached from reality Einstein appeared, despite being the godfather of physics.

He believed that once this strange conversation ended, he could eagerly focus on his future. He wanted to find his own happiness and peace of mind, focusing on the practical aspects of his earthly life rather than getting caught up in complicated philosophical puzzles.

The man nodded once again as Einstein took a step back, rested his chin on his hand, and appeared to be in a state of dilemma or confusion. His confusion wasn't mainly about finding another intangible item; He had his own galaxies of such treasures.

His main goal seemed to be finding a way to free the man from being fixated on the "M" part of the formula, the Matter. Einstein continued with disappointment, "The next item is your Bliss."

The man, tired of the conversation, glanced at Einstein in boredom and replied, "Isn't that just another way for those who haven't achieved any tangible success to hide their miseries? I don't need bliss if I have all these items in my possession."

In his free time the man planned meticulously for trips to different places around the world, and with his XYZ double down algorithm, he would have a new destination to explore almost every week of his life. "It could surpass even the notion of bliss! Who knows?" The man added arrogantly.

Einstein, feeling a bit agitated, hastily moved on to the next item. "What about Wisdom? If you were stripped of it, wouldn't you feel empty and less valuable?"

Upon hearing this, the man burst into hysterical laughter, nearly falling off the bed. He struggled to regain his composure and behave.

"Mr. Einstein! It's the 21st century! Just look around you. You keep presenting me with the most insignificant and neglected things one can imagine. If you had lived in the age of social media, surely you would offer something more valuable than 'Wisdom.' And where does wisdom even fit into all of this?"

"If I can attain a public figure-like status, then I will have access to countless sources of wisdom by default. I could become a nutritionist, sharing professional advice on what to eat and what to avoid based on my personal experiences and outcomes."

"I might even dabble in psychology, offering guidance on topics ranging from child upbringing to marriage counseling and beyond. Welcome to the entitlement era! Here, we set our own 'rules and standards' that are more about grabbing your attention than seeking your approval..."

Einstein was quite shocked by the man's high level of confidence, arrogance, and confrontational attitude. He wondered if it was worth making another attempt, given that the man dismissed all these significant losses as insignificant.

It wasn't that Einstein had such faith in rational thinking that he hesitated to present another intangible item that could magically change the man's perspective. The main reason he held back was a deep sadness in his heart.

Einstein couldn't help but reflect on his own fortune in being born in a time when rules were established based on more rational and logically accepted conventions, rather than passing trends.

He felt grateful for the genuine respect he received, and the profound interest people had in sharing his groundbreaking theories as well as his valuable life lessons. He shared those insights not as a self-proclaimed spiritual or motivational leader, but through his authentic personal stories and as a living example of humility and compassion.

In a way, he found himself appreciating the fact that he passed away long before his mind became so toughened that he couldn't even accept the existence of anything intangible, which included his own precious formulas. But above all, he would miss the blessings of intangible items that he had already experienced in his life, such as the genuine love he held for humanity...

CHAPTER 3

To Win or Not to Win?

"TO BE OR NOT TO BE" was a dilemma of the past, but today we face a different kind of puzzle, one that potentially evokes a similar level of controversy: "To win or not to win."

On one hand, we are encouraged to embrace our uniqueness and let it shine. On the other hand, greatness and success are often evaluated solely based on winning outcomes, disregarding the worth and depth of our experiences.

The path we traverse is often overlooked unless it leads to a significant winning outcome that captures attention. Even though we are exposed to countless motivational quotes urging us to disregard the opinions of others, as social beings, our perceptions of win or loss are influenced by the society we live in rather than solely by our own judgments.

Let's just take a moment to set aside the societal implications associated with the concept of "winning and losing" and focus solely on the influence of words.

Words go beyond being mere vessels of letters and sounds. They possess an extraordinary capacity to evoke emotions and shape our thoughts, feelings, and actions. They have the power to uplift and inspire us or to deflate and discourage us.

Despite their significant power, words possess a notable vulnerability or perhaps a hidden strength—they lack tangibility. Like many other intangible entities, their immediate value often goes unnoticed, and they may not receive the recognition they deserve.

In today's world, we witness the emergence of numerous NGOs dedicated to protecting and safeguarding a wide range of subjects—almost anything one can imagine.

For example, there is an NGO called "The Campaign for Dark Skies", which advocates for reducing light pollution and preserving dark skies to safeguard the visibility of stars and protect nocturnal wildlife.

Despite the existence of all these different NGOs and campaigns, it seems that relatively little attention is given to the mistreatment of certain significant entities, including abstract ones like "words" themselves.

When it comes to the misuse of words that can potentially touch on sensitive topics, we often face widespread criticism or even bear the consequences of such violations. However, when the misuse or even manipulation of specific words negatively affects the well-being of many individuals, but those words do not fall under the category of sensitive topics, it often seems that not many of us pay enough attention or show sensitivity.

What happens when the continuous misuse of words becomes a popular trend? Especially when influential figures contribute to setting these trends. One consequence is that even engaging in discussions to question the meanings of these words or seeking clarifications can lead to harsh criticism, isolation, or verbal conflicts.

Are you curious enough to explore these potentially misused words as an observer? What if we could seize the opportunity to think independently and challenge prevailing notions? Or, even more ambitiously, contribute to the restoration of these perceived abused entities?

In the era of social media, where personal branding, self-promotion, and motivational content dominate, we frequently encounter words like "winning," "success," and "greatness" at every turn.

But have you taken a moment to consider how their meanings may have undergone significant changes? Let's start dissecting some of these words and embrace the power of independent thinking.

Success:

"The achievement of a Goal or Objective."

Do you also think words like Goal or Objective can be as diverse as our DNA? Your goal is like a unique mark, specific to you, just as mine is distinct to me.

Certainly, there are specific categories or types of these different goals and objectives that have broader appeal and widespread popularity. They can include anything related to financial goals, or dreams.

It seems that the current motivational and success trends align more with these specific categories of meanings when they make contents revolving around goals and objectives.

This will ultimately result in excessive promotion of these specific meanings and categories while largely disregarding other valid alternatives, whether explicitly or implicitly.

Out of personal curiosity, I decided to conduct casual online research. I wanted to explore the various meanings of the word "success" and how it is perceived in different social media contexts over the span of one month. It's important to note that these were random observations, and no definitive conclusions can be drawn from them. However, they provided some thought-provoking results into how people commonly depict and understand success.

Irrespective of the context, the term "success" was often associated with wealth or achieving impressive business-related goals. It is worth noting that people rarely used descriptive words to specify the particular type of success they were referring to in their social media posts or quotes.

I am not sure whether, in the past, we utilized "success" with more specific adjectives to describe different forms of success, such as financial, relational, spiritual, educational, or parental, among others. Was its usage always as generic and less specific? There seems to be significant potential for researching the evolution of the meaning and usage of the word "Success" in recent decades.

This generic usage of the term "success," with an emphasis on a single aspect, presents a challenge for individuals to showcase their accomplishments in different areas to the same extent as the concept of "Unisized Success" does.

Let's reflect on this point with a practical example: Over the past decade, we have witnessed a notable rise in the number of Generation Z members attaining unprecedented levels of wealth, sometimes even before reaching the age of 18. These remarkable individuals are often recognized as highly successful and are often presented and showcased as role models or even as leaders for others to emulate.

There is no denying their financial success, whether we are comfortable to acknowledge it or not. However, simply because the term "success" is used in a generic manner, should we automatically assume that they are equally successful in other areas of their lives and readily accept them as leaders?

In reality, and through many online stories and contents where these individuals share their personal lives and struggles, it seems we better hesitate to automatically apply the label of "successful" to all aspects of their lives, as they are facing difficulties in navigating the demands of their new lifestyle and may need assistance themselves.

Some may argue that financial success carries such significance that it should be regarded as the sole definition of success.

Even if we consider that to be true, ironically, it seems that what is being promoted through these trends is not primarily the financial success itself, but rather the endorsement of a metaphorical measuring tool used to assess individuals and their personal stories as we discussed in earlier chapter.

The concept of "enough is enough" is generally accepted in most aspects of our lives when it comes to achieving a balanced existence, except in the pursuit of "Unisized Success."

If someone challenges "the more, the better" mindset, particularly on social media, they may feel pressured by prevailing trends to provide a specific and measurable benchmark or threshold of what constitutes "enough" in real-life settings.

It appears that any alternative and definitive answers primarily depend on our lifestyle, choices, and priorities, rather than a specific financial level.

Despite this seemingly straightforward answer, in heated online discussions or generally in real-life debates, when someone provide an answer to this question based on their own lifestyle or authentic dreams, they may face humiliation for holding such low standards or perspectives.

There are often misconceptions that suggest people who willingly choose a lower standard of living are unwilling to make sacrifices. But regardless of one's dreams or obsessions, sacrificing is always a necessary part of pursuing any goal or dream.

Sacrifice is always present, yet society's prevailing trends and values dictate which ones are acknowledged and rewarded, while others may not even be recognized as sacrifices.

Let's consider a sociologist who invests numerous hours in researching significant community issues due to their profound passion for making a meaningful contribution to society.

Or let's turn our attention to some parents who willingly choose to prioritize their caregiver role and allocate more time to their children, rather than working long hours or juggling multiple jobs. Their aim is to prioritize their children's overall well-being, by being more actively involved.

These examples are merely a few among the countless sacrifices that exist beyond the scope of this book. These sacrifices, along with similar ones, are often undervalued and unrecognized.

In some cases, these sacrifices have even encountered ridicule when they were discussed and labeled as sacrifice. An unfortunate example that I observed on social media involved an influential figure who openly ridiculed parents who prioritize attending their children's school games. Rather than acknowledging the commitment and sacrifices these parents make to support their children emotionally, he dismissed it as an insignificant obsession.

Now, let's pause for a moment and reflect: When we consume current motivational contents how frequently do we associate their use of the word "sacrifice" and "hard work" with pursuits other than financial or business goals?

Do they serve as a reminder of the sacrifices of such parents and similar ones? Or do we primarily interpret them as messages urging us to sacrifice our time for multiple side hustles and pursue larger financial goals?

An iconic leader, whom I have been following for over two decades, efficiently conveyed this notion with some practical examples that excessive focus on one area of life often comes at the expense of sacrificing other aspects. He emphasized that it is unrealistic to expect to excel equally in all areas of life.

So, when "Unisized Success" trends promote a biased outlook on what should be considered as sacrifice, some people cannot help but feel that their efforts were wasted.

They may look back with regret on all the time and energy they invested in prioritizing alternative definitions of success. It is disheartening for them to realize that those countless hours and endeavors cannot be easily translated into tangible outcomes that align with the standards of "Unisized Success."

I have come across contents and posts where some influential figures, occasionally made efforts to "redefine success."

Based on my personal experience, their handling of opposing comments and their unwillingness to engage in open discussions showed that such attempts were primarily motivated by their desire to seek attention, which they frequently referred to as their number one asset.

If an individual lacks the ability to handle opposition on a smaller scale and consistently exhibits retaliatory behaviors across various platforms, it raises doubts about their qualifications to redefine such concepts on a global level.

You have likely come across the 80/20 rule, also known as the Pareto Principle. Essentially, it states that approximately 80% of the outcomes or results come from roughly 20% of the causes or efforts. This principle is often used to illustrate how inputs and outputs are unevenly distributed in various aspects of life, such as business, productivity, and time management.

Interestingly, it appears that such influential figures may consciously or subconsciously employ this strategy as their primary tactic when promoting the concept of "Celebritized Greatness-Unisized Success", their "Vital Few", based on the rule.

However, they never want to optimize these vital few, since in a modern society that emphasizes freedom of speech and equality among individuals, who would pay attention to someone confidently asserting, "I am superior to you because of my 'Unisized Success' status, so do not question what I say or face the consequences?" Such audacity undoubtedly elicits immediate reactions and creates distance between the speaker and the audience or potentially leads to more significant consequences.

So, by concentrating on promoting concepts such as kindness, humility, and workplace culture in approximately 80% of their content, they will capture the attention of a broad audience. However, when the opportune moment arises, they subtly introduce the remaining 20%of their message—the promotion of "Celebritized Greatness-Unisized Success."

At this point, we observe frequent examples that extremely offensive language and dark sarcasm are utilized to characterize or refer to individuals who choose to live a less ambitious life or who are not actively involved in activities similar to theirs.

By embodying the concept of "Celebritized Greatness" they firmly believe they have the right to treat people, concepts, and alternative ideas in such a manner.

They may perceive it as their divine mission to make people uncomfortable in order to facilitate personal growth. However, when they are confronted with opposing ideas that make them uncomfortable, the domino effect of unprofessionalism starts immediately.

Despite these controversial behaviors, they continue to actively participate in cultural and educational movements. One possible reason why this happens on such a wide scale, even influencing the elites of society who unquestioningly follow their lead, could be attributed to these individuals' vague "Why I am here?" stories.

If "serving others" is not an individual's primary motivation when answering such questions, there is a strong likelihood that they will prioritize themselves and their personal brand over the truth when confronted with criticism, controversy, or challenging questions.

It is undeniable that not everyone possesses the inherent selflessness demonstrated by Mother Teresa, as we all have our own financial obligations to fulfill. However, it is during these challenging moments that we are compelled to make difficult choices that reflect our true values.

In the realm of success and motivation, not only are these "Why I am here?" stories often insufficiently unfolded, but there is also a tendency to share distorted and exaggerated accounts in response to such questions.

This can potentially cultivate a blind trust that may result in negative consequences for the audience, including feelings of disappointment, unrealistic expectations, and confusion.

As mere observers in our everyday lives, not only do we refrain from questioning their "Why I am here?" narratives, but we also, under the influence of their grand endorsements, tend to automatically dismiss any doubts regarding their stories.

Instead of observing, engaging in critical thinking, and seeking clarification, we often opt for the safer path of trust and compliance. This approach can have a negative impact on our independent thinking and result in blindly following their lead.

Consequently, when public figures express viewpoints that contradict our own observations, logic, science, or established facts, we often find ourselves hesitant to openly share our own perspectives.

We find ourselves being largely packed as average and ordinary, with many aspects of our lives still in question or progress, including our own levels of greatness, success, identity, self-esteem, self-confidence, and self-worth.

One aspect that is often overlooked is our level of knowledge. Regardless of how much we know, if we have not achieved that "Unisized Success" status, we run the risk of facing harsh ostracism. Instead of being listened to and welcomed into meaningful conversations, we encounter the metaphorical sword of "Who are you?" or "How dare you?" slashing down upon us.

CHAPTER 4

From Wins to Dreams

WHEN WAS THE LAST TIME someone said, "I have a dream," and it brought about lasting, positive change for a large group of people?

It seems that nowadays, our "I have a dream" will soon fade away, transforming into "I had a dream," which was taken away from me and replaced by someone else's dream.

Perhaps that is the reason we less frequently witness monumental positive transformations occurring in our societies. Creativity has been replaced by unified expectations, and genuine dreams, if not ridiculed, are often regarded as yet another form of delusion.

Have you ever paused to think about this remarkable fact that within the small space of our fingertips each of us possesses unique patterns? Isn't it fascinating? Billions of distinct patterns confined within such a small space, all formed by utilizing limited lines and shapes.

Why can't the same be applied to our dreams? Why can't we be equally unique in that regard? What does it even mean to "dream big" in the context of "Unisized Success"? Solely more ambitious XYZs for ourselves?

It appears that leveling also applies to our dreams. The "Celebritized Greatness-Unisized Success" trends have left their footprints even in defining the standards of our dreams.

Dream house, dream car, dream vacation... How frequently do we encounter these clichés on social media? The images and videos associated with these dreams often portray lavish and exotic destinations that appear unattainable for the majority of the audience.

But what if someone's dream house is simply a small cottage in a remote area? A place where they can breathe in fresh air, far from the chaos, crowds, and noise. Can such a dream even hold relevance in the context of today's trends of greatness and success?

Wouldn't it be surprising to see a picture of such a humble cottage in one of those motivational videos, while the speaker passionately discusses the concept of having a big dream?

So, the notion of dreaming small or big implies that the levels have already been determined, and we should conform to what has already been deemed as big or small-sized dreams. The more materialistically ambitious the dream, the larger and more significant it is perceived to be.

Conversely, if it possesses fewer such attributes, it is often regarded as a “small” dream, potentially seen as more suitable for individuals who have already been labeled as such numerous times in the contents created by these influential figures.

It seems that in the present era, individuals’ personal dreams are up for sale, aiming to achieve a specific level of “Unisized Success-Celebritized Greatness” in return.

The process of dream replacement, or even its more subtle manifestations, is unlikely to occur quickly or effortlessly. So, what causes these widespread patterns?

This question encouraged me to casually explore the underlying causes and potential consequences if this trend carries on at a massive level.

As an observer, I noticed that during the initial stages of this dream replacement process, personal dreams that deviate from the standards of “Celebritized Greatness-Unisized Success” are frequently met with criticism, humiliation, or even ridicule.

A dream is called a dream because, at its core, it is perceived as greater and more appealing than a person’s current reality. Dreams are meant to inspire us as we visualize them, giving us confidence that their realization will bring us happiness and pride.

However, if our dreams are perceived as insignificant or even absurd by the public, it can diminish our initial enthusiasm to pursue them. Individuals may even be labeled as less capable or idle simply because they did not set higher standards for their dreams based on current trends.

These drawbacks raise doubts about whether such original dreams can genuinely energize and fulfill individuals. The things that were once inspiring, and significant now appear trivial or merely ordinary aspects of their life.

This poses a challenge for them to take pride in their dreams and, most importantly, to actively pursue them. Ultimately, all these challenges may lead to deep discontentment or even resentment towards their authentic dreams.

At this point, it may seem that people's unique dreams will wither and vanish forever, leaving them to quietly live lives empty of any dreams. However, the story does not intend to end here, as individuals without dreams lack the motivation to pursue anything, including seeking "Motivation" itself.

Therefore, it becomes necessary to present alternative dreams. These alternative dreams are implanted in the minds and hearts of individuals through various means, including passionate lectures as well as popular images and videos that portray the extravagant lifestyles and manifestations of "Celebritized Greatness-Unisized Success."

Due to the constant exposure to such visual stimuli on social media, replacing individuals' fading dreams with more globally accepted alternatives is not a challenging task. With the extensive promotion and widespread availability of these alternative options, it becomes relatively effortless for individuals to find something to conform to.

Now the question arises: Why would someone's dream be replaced in the first place? Why would some people invest a significant amount of their time and resources to support multiple steps of this dream replacement process?

I prefer not to base my discussion on conspiracy theories or adopt a pessimistic stance. It is probable that all these perceived processes and steps mentioned above occur unintentionally, simply as a result of biased outlooks and personal preferences.

However, it is difficult to overlook such pervasive commercialization of personal dreams that is taking place.

Similar to personal stories, if everyone is obsessed with their own dreams and striving to bring them to realization, who would have the time to seek out role models and invest a significant amount of their time and resources in mirroring their paths to success and greatness?

There are numerous patterns, where the dedication of "Dream Followers" brings immense financial gain and fame to those who sell these dreams. This could be evident through increased sales of their product lines or any affiliation they have, as well as the proliferation of their courses or seminars promising to open the very door, they themselves had the chance to unlock.

Embracing the Intangible More

With the rapid advancement of the Internet and technology, the landscape of our human existence has undergone significant transformations compared to decades ago, both for better and for worse. Concepts that were previously defined and evaluated based on traditional standards have been fundamentally reshaped.

In an era where individuals devote substantial time and resources to social media platforms and virtual reality, could new horizons and dimensions be considered for the current understanding of human rights? So, it can more effectively address a broader range of incidents involving online human rights violations.

While I am not an expert by any means and have limited information on this matter, it appears that there are noteworthy ongoing movements and campaigns advocating for such expansions.

In general, real-world events are typically regarded as more significant than online occurrences. However, ironically, it seems that the online world is the actual place where the main trends are shaped and dominate our physical reality.

If we were to hypothetically place a person with physical or mental challenges on the street and witness them being insulted due to their shortcomings, many individuals would likely respond promptly and with great resolve to defend them. However, if a similar situation occurs in the online world, meaningful actions are often absent.

To provide a specific example, I have witnessed an ongoing situation where a neurodiverse person's story has been subjected to consistent ridicule and bullying on multiple social media pages as a part of unprofessional retaliatory actions.

I regularly visited those pages to monitor the comments and observe the patterns of reactions regarding this sensitive topic. Almost none of the tens of thousands of followers showed any sensitivity towards these types of posts or comments, or the instances of such reactions were so rare that they could be considered practically non-existent.

In similar cases, the primary issue appears to be the inadequate oversight by responsible entities within those social media platforms which can reflect a relative lack of concern for human rights in the online world.

Now, let's consider another example to get a better grasp of the issue. Just imagine UNICEF workers who are bringing food to hungry children, each child pleading for their only meal of the day. The agony and misery in their dimly lit eyes due to starvation, reveal the depths of their despair. One can sense their pain and suffering in every movement as they desperately try to reach the bowl even a few seconds faster.

At that very moment, imagine someone rushes toward a volunteer and forcefully knocks the bowl from their hand. The tear-filled eyes of the starving child, looking around in despair, seem to blame that cruel person and all the bystanders for his hunger.

Now, let's explore a similar scenario on social media.

As always, somewhere in the world, for various reasons, a group of children are experiencing hunger and hardship. They urgently need food to alleviate their immediate suffering and avoid starvation.

In response to certain posts addressing this issue, I have noticed some very harsh comments suggesting that children are destined to suffer along with other inappropriate language that I cannot quote here.

These comments aimed to downplay the significance of these charitable efforts and portrayed them as unimportant and boastful.

They suggested that engaging in such small actions is ineffective and lacks the potential to have a substantial lasting impact on the pervasive issues of child labor and starvation.

It is similar to saying, "Why bother feeding myself or my children? We will just get hungry again soon." Hunger remains a constant throughout life, yet it does not prevent us from nourishing ourselves daily.

It is puzzling why similar acts of online cruelty fail to generate similar assertive responses as they do in real-life situations. Perhaps it is because they lack a sense of tangibility.

When we read such extreme comments, we cannot hear the sound of a bowl hitting the ground, witness the spilled meal, or experience the desperation, crying, and screaming of an innocent child. We also cannot perceive the level of shock and disbelief felt by a UNICEF hero witnessing such cruelty.

This pervasive lack of empathy exhibited in some online interactions can give rise to and create highly unfavorable trends. Online harm, online bullying and abuse are prevalent, whether we are willing to admit it or not.

In today's online world, it may appear that we all have an equal opportunity to voice our opinions and observations. However, many individuals are not granted permission to get on the "Attention Bus" due to their disapproval of the prevailing trends.

Imagine if Rosa Parks technically had the option to sit in the front seat, but in reality, the front seats symbolized online retaliation, dehumanization, degradation, and complete ignorance by those who are driving the attention bus. As a result, moving to the back seat was the only seemingly free choice for her to make.

The struggle is not an explicit confrontation, but a subtle ongoing battle based on individual's primary values and beliefs. If someone were to stand up and say, "I am not allowed to sit in the front seat, not because of my race, but because of my dream or personal story" they would most likely be perceived as someone out of their mind who may need professional help...

CHAPTER 5

Self-Worth and Identity in Action

Self-Worth in Action

THERE ARE NUMEROUS RESOURCES available, both by experts and amateurs, that explore the intricate concept of self-worth. They also explore how our comprehension of this subject can profoundly impact our mental and physical well-being and our overall happiness and fulfillment in life.

While the abundance of published material on the topic undoubtedly provides valuable insights and perspectives, let's "momentarily" set aside any preexisting notions as well as the guidance offered by mentors and motivational figures on these topics.

Instead, let's fully engage with the real world, where the weight and influence of inspirational quotes have limited impact over the tangible measures of worth imposed by prevailing trends. Let's roll up our sleeves and take a closer look at the concept of self-worth through the lens of an observer in everyday life.

To truly understand what "Self-Worth in Action" means, we need to break it down and examine the term "self-worth." In simple terms, self-worth refers to "how we perceive our own value". Now, let's explore the most controversial word in this phrase: "Value."

Value is defined as "The level at which someone or something deserves to be valued or rated." So, the essential question would be: What are these levels of value and/or how they are determined?

As human beings, we are believed to possess inherent value. Yet, it is important to analyze and understand how this inherent value is influenced and to some extent defined within the social contexts.

In various motivational and self-help resources, it is often suggested that individuals have the ability to independently define their level of value or worth, regardless of the context that surrounds them.

While this guidance may appear empowering and captivating, it is important to bear in mind that our discussion revolves around real-life situations in which the influence of societal expectations, experiences, and the opinions of others cannot be easily disregarded.

We are examining the practicality of implementing such advice in everyday life, going beyond their role as mere engaging phrases confined to yoga sessions or morning routines.

Despite the excess of such motivational advice, societal expectations often align more closely with the current trends of "Celebritized Greatness-Unisized Success" when defining these levels of value.

For a brief moment, we can even set aside these prevailing trends and their impact and delve into a hypothetical scenario within a utopian context.

In such a world, we can envision a value system that aligns more closely with human nature, defining the worth of individuals more in harmony with insights from psychology, sociology or other relevant knowledge and wisdom, rather than being predominantly influenced by popular culture.

In these scientific fields, human beings are considered as multi-faceted creatures and have different dimensions that extend beyond the physical realm.

Recognizing this multi-dimensional nature presents challenges when attempting to establish levels based solely on a single dimension or, even worse, based only on the current trends.

Let's imagine a person who has wholeheartedly dedicated themselves to nurturing their spiritual aspect. They have focused on developing personal values by focusing on connecting with something greater than themselves. Their total commitment to their spiritual dimension may potentially have resulted in some supernatural abilities, similar to those of the renowned yogis.

However, they have totally neglected their physical well-being. So, they experience a noticeable decline in muscle strength and overall health. They also have overlooked their family and young children, failing to provide the necessary support.

These sacrifices have been made in the pursuit of uninterrupted mindfulness practice for extended periods of time.

Considering these circumstances, it raises questions about whether this person can accurately assess their self-worth based solely on their spiritual dimension, especially if that is the only dimension they prioritize.

Let's consider that this person indeed evaluates his value solely based on this dimension. While this perspective may bring him extreme joy and contentment within his isolated social context, as observers, we may question the accuracy of his self-assessment.

In our own assessment of this person, we may consider multiple dimensions beyond the spiritual one. Their lack of progress and achievements in other areas of life may significantly influence how we perceive and value this person in various social contexts.

So, defining one's worth solely based on a single dimension may not accurately reflect an individual's true self-worth. It also does not guarantee that others will perceive and treat them accordingly.

In the field of psychology, extensive research has been carried out on the influence of external factors on self-worth. Social psychology, in particular, examines how societal expectations, cultural norms, interpersonal relationships, and feedback from others can influence an individual's sense of self-worth.

These insights highlight the intricate interplay between internal perceptions and external influences in shaping an individual's ultimate definitions of their value and self-worth. So, it may not simply be an internal game as self-help content often perceive and suggest.

Yet, simply recognizing human beings as multi-dimensional, does not automatically guarantee that we will be evaluated based on all these aspects in our day-to-day interactions or in broader social contexts.

In practice, or as referred to in this chapter as "in Action," people are frequently assessed based on a few, if not just one or two, immediately noticeable dimensions.

Some individuals may argue that since we cannot fully comprehend all the dimensions of a person unless we share a deep connection with them, it becomes necessary to find a way to evaluate, or assess individuals based on the dimensions that are readily observable to us.

Even if we acknowledge the validity of this argument and agree to base our judgments solely on dimensions that are visible or easily noticeable, such as the physical and social aspects, it is important to question the criteria and levels in these areas and how they are established.

When it comes to our physical bodies, which play a significant role in our physical dimension, have we ever paused to consider who establishes the criteria by which people often value themselves or are valued and judged?

It is hard to ignore how beauty standards have changed over time, especially in the past couple of decades, often focusing on a small group of famous people with similar body shapes. This has resulted in everyday individuals resorting to injections, body sculpting, and rigorous workouts in hopes of conforming to these standards.

In contrast to pre-social media times, these patterns go beyond a simple interest in fashion; they have become all-consuming obsessions with these standards, fueled by the prevailing trends.

People are taking extreme measures to keep up with these standards, and this can have a detrimental effect on their physical and mental well-being.

Instances of unhealthy diets leading to starvation, risky surgeries, and even fatal outcomes serve as clear examples that the current standards or criteria in our physical dimension may not necessarily align with the ultimate human potential in this dimension.

This reflects what I previously referred to as "Celebritized Greatness." It demonstrates how this concept is utilized to establish new benchmarks for evaluating our greatness and worth across various dimensions, including our physical dimension.

With these trends being promoted on a global scale, it becomes increasingly challenging for less captivating educational programs or parental advice to effectively counteract their influence.

By prioritizing popular culture and such trends as the determining factors of value and greatness across various dimensions of human life, rather than embracing what is genuinely healthy, worthwhile, and balanced based on science, knowledge, collective awareness, or even our common sense, we may expose ourselves to potentially irreversible negative consequences.

In today's world, the fear we once held about a single person or group seizing control and dominating everything seems less significant. Yet, it is worth considering the potential for lasting adverse changes resulting from "Celebritized Greatness-Unisized Success" trends.

Would giving in to these trends have any less impact than the consequences faced in major historical conflicts? Regardless of the answer, perhaps each of us carries a certain responsibility to contribute, both in small and significant ways, to ensure that we are genuinely advancing along the path of human evolution and not moving in the opposite direction.

Identity in Action

Just as with self-worth, despite the numerous insightful resources available on identity, the aim here is to explore this concept "in Action", examining how the discussed current trends will impact our sense of self.

Our identities, like self-worth, have both internal and external aspects. Our experiences, achievements, setbacks, challenges, and relationships all contribute to how we perceive ourselves.

No matter how impressive and valuable we regard the main character of our story, our identity, to be, its significance diminishes when it is detached from the context of societal norms, values, and standards.

If our identities do not align with widely accepted notions within a society or community, we may even hesitate to perceive ourselves as the main characters in our own narratives.

When individuals are seen as losers, insignificant, or unworthy by default based on the prevailing trends, they may choose to play the victim role in their personal narratives.

They assign the "main character role" to external factors such as adversities, circumstances, or other obstacles that prevented them from achieving the "Unisized Success".

Despite the abundance of motivational messages emphasizing individuality and self-acceptance, only certain types of identities align with the standards of "Celebritized Greatness-Unisized Success."

Consequently, we observe numerous messages that encourage us to alter or reshape our identities to possess the qualities deemed necessary for achieving "Unisized Success."

This dynamic results in a gradual erosion of individuals' unique identities. These expectations and demands slowly chip away at their authentic sense of self.

Given the pervasive existence of such perspectives and trends, it is not unrealistic to imagine a future where a nearly flawless AI-generated humanoid could seamlessly replace a human without anyone experiencing a sense of lack or absence.

As individuality is disregarded and people are encouraged to mold their identities to conform to such trends, the likelihood of finding ourselves in a world dominated by robotic humans or humanoid robots seems to increase significantly.

Now, let's informally explore identity at a broader scale such as workplace and communities.

What unfolds within the confines of office cubicles across various industries can reflect, to some extent, the work culture of a society.

There is a commonly held belief that as AI technology continues to advance, the necessity of individuals engaged in repetitive office tasks will diminish.

Some people perceive these employees as the ones who are simply waiting for retirement and making limited contributions to the economy. As a result, they welcome the idea of AI relieving businesses from the burden of employing a large workforce in such roles.

Despite the ongoing debates, it remains uncertain whether a widespread transition to an AI workforce in corporate jobs will occur soon. After all, it is challenging to compare the task of cleaning restrooms by robots to the complexity of managing multiple intricate spreadsheets and engaging in multitasking to complete various activities.

It seems society still relies on these office jobs for its day-to-day operations. So, it is important to recognize and address any challenges that come with them to ensure the well-being of employees and maintain a healthy economy.

Now, we may ask whether it is solely the matter of low pay and other low standards of corporate jobs that turns many employees into seemingly robotic beings, eagerly counting down the days until Friday and constantly seeking ways to escape from their jobs.

Is the main problem the pervasive workplace culture that overlooks their worth as valuable contributors to the broader picture of prosperity and success? Or is it the lack of respect that ultimately drives them to seek recognition and value elsewhere?

Based on my personal experience, and considering the shared sentiments of others, both in real life and on social media, it seems that the prevailing culture within corporate environments is often the primary source of this discontent.

The main idea here is not to imply that job satisfaction alone is the primary factor that prevents people from quitting their jobs for better opportunities or to start their own businesses.

Many individuals choose to change jobs in pursuit of more favorable work environments or better career prospects. However, it seems that the dissatisfaction and lack of full commitment to their current job often stem from the unfavorable corporate culture, rather than solely being driven by a genuine desire for personal growth and career advancement.

It is intriguing to consider the terminology that society applies to categorize these individuals. The term "rat race" itself captures many aspects of how this group is often perceived and undervalued.

The term is generally understood to show the competitive and relentless pursuit of material success and social status in modern society.

However, nowadays it seems that the phrase is being used for a rather contradictory purpose. It has mainly become a way to label non-ambitious individuals in corporate jobs who are content with modest rewards that impedes their motivation and discourages them from actively pursuing "Unisized Success."

Additionally, the rigid criteria for both greatness and success in current trends does not align with the lifestyle of typical 9-5 workers. The perceived gap between their current status and what these trends require them to be, often makes it impossible for them to believe that they too can be considered Great. This significant distance creates a profound sense of discouragement and disbelief.

I remember a relevant incident when I shared some of my goals and the practical steps I was taking to escape corporate life with a few colleagues. Instead of any curiosity or support, I faced ridicule and humiliation through direct and indirect messages. They made remarks like, "We small people..." or "There is no elevator to success, you have to take the stairs," and similar expressions reflecting their limiting mindset and disbelief.

This trapped hamster identity born out of constant frustration, can ultimately compromise the employees' sense of dignity and make life more challenging not only for themselves but also for those who dare to seek an escape or believe in their own potential and capabilities.

As a result, the workplace culture can become unhealthy, characterized by backstabbing, gossip, or a general lack of empathy towards colleagues. This poisonous dynamic is commonly referred to as a "Toxic Workplace" in numerous social media contents.

When the sense of community and unity deteriorates, employees may find themselves surrendering power to management and accepting compromises and unfair treatment as their new standard. This may occur because they no longer have the support and solidarity of their peers in such situations.

The presence of such evident toxic culture can further strengthen the sense of authority and embolden those in power to exhibit such attitudes without fear of consequences.

This could be one of the reasons why, even in the most democratic societies, we witness the rise and persistence of ego-centric identities within smaller communities such as the workplace.

In the long run, this culture can have an adverse effect on employees' mental well-being and productivity, which can ultimately have similar harmful impacts on society overall.

Another way that prevailing trends may affect the concept of identity is how it leads to an increased consumerist identity and its drastic effects on the lives of these average and ordinary people.

When authentic identities lose their significance in gaining recognition in various social settings, individuals often resort to imitating the superficial facade of greatness and give in to "instant gratification."

This may help to explain the root cause of the widespread impulsive shopping habits, living beyond one's means, excessive debt, and maxed-out credit cards.

In self-help and motivational contents, the criticism of instant gratification and impulsive spending habits is a recurring theme. However, not many of them truly emphasize how the prevailing trends promote and provoke such behaviors.

CHAPTER 6

Constructive Disruptions

Greater Inclusivity

MANY INFLUENTIAL FIGURES and leaders often seem to believe that they are destined to solve the major problems of society. As a result, they most often provide generic, one-size-fits-all solutions.

But isn't it true that the overarching issues faced by society primarily stem from the problems experienced by individuals within that society?

Perhaps, instead of solely focusing on large-scale transformations at the macro level, a more sustainable solution lies in identifying and investing in genuine problems faced by individuals.

In this book, we have explored several ways in which the concept of "Celebritized Greatness-Unisized Success" fails to resonate with the diverse experiences of different groups of people and it can even jeopardize their mental and social well-being at times.

Those who promote these trends utilize various methods, leveraging their influence to capture widespread attention. Consequently, countering or reversing these powerful trends poses a significant challenge. However, if we genuinely believe in the power of hope, there must exist counteracting forces capable of balancing the attention.

But where do we truly desire the attention to be directed?

Maybe it is fair to allocate some of that attention to valuable areas that have been overlooked or underrepresented due to the excessive promotion of such trends.

The life stories that have been unfairly evaluated and permanently silenced. The genuine narratives of personal growth, meaningful relationships, and even lesser-recognized positive contributions to communities, all deserve our attention in one way or another.

Typically, the aim of most online content, at a very basic level, is to capture attention, whether it involves sharing a simple household trick or showcasing a cutting-edge robotic innovation. Once attention is captured, it can then be redirected or converted for advertising, sales, or other purposes.

But how frequently do we observe something deviating from this norm for a different purpose? How often do we actively seek unconverted attention solely for the purpose of capturing it?

It is similar to encountering a situation where you notice someone on the street who is about to fall into a hole, and you urgently divert their attention to the impending danger. In that moment, all that matters is their undivided focus, even if you never cross paths with that person in your lifetime.

While social media occasionally features videos showcasing authentic moments and spontaneous acts, they often fade into the background when compared to the dominance of contents centered around popular trends.

Although I lack adequate social skills and more strategic plans to make a major impact, I have taken a small step in shifting attention towards a more inclusive perspective on greatness and success within my abilities.

So, I have created an Instagram page, @Redefinebyastory, as a platform for individuals to share their diverse stories and perspectives on success and greatness, enabling me to reflect on and uplift their stories.

Contributors can share contents in any format, shedding light on various aspects and definitions of success and greatness, whether through their own stories, everyday life examples, or those of others.

The intention is not necessarily to redefine these terms, but rather to draw attention to the often-overlooked aspects and manifestations of success and greatness.

Collaboration

To redirect attention towards more inclusive trends, another effective strategy may be the collaboration between younger and older generations in creating content.

Despite the popularity of younger generations' content and its ability to attract widespread attention, it may not provide an accurate portrayal of the actual challenges experienced by millions of individuals in their daily lives. These challenges extend to many different areas, including health, interpersonal relationships, financial stability, and other aspects of everyday life struggles.

A productive collaboration between creative young individuals and seasoned older generations, who bring valuable knowledge and expertise, seems like a win-win situation. They can support each other, much like two people working together— one, often associated with wisdom and experience, and the other, typically marked by fresh perspectives and innovative ideas.

Due to their fast-paced lifestyle and shorter attention spans, younger generations may encounter challenges in conducting thorough research and fact-checking, which are sometimes necessary to provide more accurate content.

As a result, these characteristics often lead to numerous instances of inaccurately attributing statements such as "Scientific studies show..." or "Research shows..." or similar broadly used phrases to gain credibility.

By encouraging collaboration between these two groups, there is an opportunity to redirect attention towards healthier trends and cultivate a more diverse and balanced perspective on success, greatness, and health-related content.

For instance, individuals who have achieved remarkable success, in their long-lasting marriages, even up until their 70s, are often overlooked when it comes to providing practical relationship advice. On the other hand, a young person in their 20s or 30s who has achieved a "Unisized Success" status can quickly gain recognition as a guru in many areas, offering bold statements based on their personal and often limited experience in relationships.

We even come across posts from these influencers who suggest to their audience to envision their partners as mere household items or possessions, offering relationship advice based on that perspective.

Wouldn't it be healthier for society if these individuals felt a sense of responsibility rather than an impulse to offer advice on a wide range of topics mainly out of entitlement?

They should consider how their guidance on such topics may be disconnected from the reality of someone seeking a more authentic type of relationship based on different values than the prevailing trends.

Instead of offering such bold quotes, these individuals can provide their personal perspective on a specific relationship concept. They can then actively seek out the viewpoints and insights of older individuals with successful relationships by conducting occasional online interviews or simply sharing these senior's advice in their posts and content.

Diversity in leadership

The concept of being "laser-focused," often mentioned in motivational content, is valuable for goal setting and eliminating distractions on the path to success. But can we apply this concept to leadership itself? Should we be similarly focused when choosing whom to listen to and follow?

We have embraced broad labels like "success coach" or "mentor," assuming that their advice should universally apply to everyone, irrespective of age, mindset, background, goals, professions, and other factors.

It does not seem practical to expect leaders who have a strong preference or inclination towards a specific definition of success to effectively inspire a diverse group of people with different priorities especially when their contents also do not address the diverse needs and concerns of their team or followers.

Having a varied range of motivational leaders seems to be crucial, as they not only provide motivation but also inspire appropriate actions among their followers.

When influential leaders, whether intentionally or unintentionally, promote the "Celebritized Greatness-Unisized Success" trends based on their personal preference, it often results in followers prioritizing actions more aligned with that type of greatness and success.

This consistency in obsessively advocating something may be viewed as advantageous particularly for followers who prioritize "Unisized Success" above all else.

However, it can be misleading and disappointing when considering the diverse range of individuals consuming this generic content. The one-size-fits-all approach fails to acknowledge the varying needs and priorities of the audience members.

For instance, teenagers may perceive success as effectively managing their time between studying, playing games, and using social media. They may also desire a clear plan of action to achieve this age-specific type of success in their lives. It is unlikely that leaders who primarily target adult audiences would adequately address such specific topics in their speeches.

In the absence or insufficiency of such age-specific mentors on social media, it is not uncommon to see individuals with “Unisized Success” status, take it upon themselves to create educational storybooks for children.

While it is true that anyone is free to create storybooks for children, only a select few individuals possess the widespread recognition and influence necessary for their work to reach a broad audience. As a result, these influential figures have the power to shape and promote trends that reflect their personal values and priorities, aiming to instill these perspectives in future generations.

Moreover, why should kids and teenagers be subjected to motivational speakers who consistently use highly inappropriate language and frequently exhibit aggressive behavior?

It appears that even certain teenagers who have achieved success in finding a balance and reaching their age-specific goals could serve as better role models in creating motivational contents to support and inspire their peers.

Indeed, there are many articulate, and capable adolescents who may have already begun providing such contents. However, due to the insufficiency of these role models, they are unable to adequately meet the demand of this large demographic.

Similarly, the need for more targeted leadership applies to different career groups. As one of the most demanding professions, individuals in the healthcare industry, regardless of their rank or role, whether they are nightshift nurses or top surgeons, require motivational content that directly addresses the specific challenges of their jobs.

Can we practically expect these professionals to be adequately motivated by generic motivational content alone, to the extent that they would abandon their valuable careers and pursue entrepreneurship? Or should they instead seek motivational content that specifically acknowledges their unique challenges and emphasizes the values of their profession, inspiring them to persist rather than yield?

This approach may help these individuals to find a sense of contentment and fulfillment as they thrive in their challenging roles. It not only addresses their concerns about the meaningfulness of the challenges and perceived lack of rewarding outcomes compared to entrepreneurial endeavors but also serves as a regular reminder of the high level of respect and value they hold in society and how vital their existence is to almost everyone.

Not long ago, I came across a YouTube ad featuring a doctor who proudly shared his noteworthy achievement of leaving his healthcare profession to start a new entrepreneurial venture. He explicitly expressed that this transition helped him evade burnout, fatigue, financial limitations, and other hardships he previously faced as a doctor and enabled him to earn a substantial income without much hassle.

While everyone can make their own choices, what was concerning was the doctor's perspective on his profession.

He evaluated the significance of being a healthcare provider solely based on financial gains and rewards, without expressing any regret for his diminished or lost ability to serve and save lives as before.

The concept of "Unisized Success" seems to be promoting similar transitions by consistently prioritizing the end result over the journey and core values.

I doubt that a couple of decades ago, a physician would openly express such joy about leaving their profession and describe it as an ongoing burden, particularly on a public platform such as YouTube, without mentioning a single blessing associated with their job.

Now, let's consider stay-at-home moms as another example. It is worth thinking about how many of them would find a sense of peace and fulfillment by engaging with current motivational trends.

It seems they may perceive generic motivational content focused on "Unisized Success-Celebritized Greatness" as more of a punishment than encouragement.

Such content often emphasizes the skills and qualities these individuals may lack or did not have the opportunity or time to develop for various reasons. Consequently, it can make them feel inadequate because they may believe that it is unlikely, if not to say impossible for them to be recognized as successful or great according to such standards.

Moreover, the goals presented in such content are often either irrelevant or do not align with the life situations of this group.

While there is an abundance of cooking or household chores videos readily available, there is a shortage of personal development speakers in this field who dedicate a significant portion of their content to inspiring and motivating this group.

Some people may skeptically question whether stay-at-home moms truly requires motivation and what its purpose would be.

It is difficult to understand how these people fail to recognize the vital role of these moms in nurturing the mental and physical well-being of their children, who contribute significantly to shaping the future of any society.

Unfortunately, there is a shortage of easily understandable and more customized resources for self-improvement, parenting advice, and nutritional guidance that can assist this group in fulfilling their responsibilities more effectively.

It seems many women in this group, particularly those with better financial resources, are influenced by the concept of "Celebritized Greatness" in a detrimental way.

They relentlessly pursue Physical attractiveness as a means to catch a glimpse of that greatness. They often prioritize cosmetic surgeries and other methods to conform to societal standards of greatness, believing it to be the only path available to them.

Island Metaphor

Picture yourself on a deserted island, completely isolated from the outside world. This island is rather large and has evidence of previous inhabitants, but it is now empty.

In the past, there were rich, middle-class, and poor individuals living together, creating a diverse society. As you explore the island, you come across different types of houses—a mix of simple houses, mansions, and humble shacks.

Traces of different lifestyles can be seen in the scattered cars. There are luxurious, fast cars, as well as average ones and old, worn-out vehicles. These items reflect the varied lives and dreams that once existed in this now deserted area.

The wrecked cars and shacks are easily usable since they have been left unlocked and abandoned, requiring no effort or hassle to use them. However, accessing the simple houses and cars poses a greater challenge because the doors are locked, and there are other obstacles to overcome.

Reaching the modern houses would involve dealing with complex security systems and putting yourself at risk of harm.

Just imagine living alone on this island-Which type of items would you prefer to choose?

It seems unlikely that many people would choose the most challenging options. The reasoning behind selecting a fast car becomes less relevant on an island where any car automatically becomes the fastest since there are no other vehicles on the road.

In such a lonely environment, availability and comfort seems to take priority over glamour and quality.

While there is nothing inherently wrong with owning and collecting beautiful and valuable things, their significance often stems from comparing them to others in our social environment, rather than having an intrinsic ability to reflect our potential.

Just as with the term "success," in personal development contents, the word "potential" is used as a generic and overarching term.

When it comes to obtaining luxurious personal possessions or setting goals to acquire more, it is important to consider that it can be a personal choice and preference. Acquiring such belongings may not necessarily serve as benchmarks for evaluating our full potential as human beings, despite what these prevailing trends suggest.

This perspective that considers the accumulations of such objects as a path to reach one's full potential can lead to inaccurate if not to say misleading motivational content.

With this mindset comes a rather unhealthy sense of entitlement, where some financially successful individuals perceive themselves as superhuman and, in a way, sacred. However, in reality, they often display a bitter and one-dimensional character.

Just to provide a tangible example of this entitlement in the online world, I recently watched an episode where an individual, a leader in the self-help industry, who has achieved one of the highest levels of "Unisized Success" was being interviewed.

It seemed his "Why I am here?" story was to toughen people's mind in pursuit of their dreams.

In a relatively brief online episode, he used profanity almost a hundred times and exhibited almost no signs of warmth or positive gestures, but rather a profound sense of melancholy.

Yet he challenged people with opposing perspectives to a debate. Would anyone even dare to take part in such a challenge? With such an offensive and defensive approach, it is unlikely that many would want to be subjected to it unless they adopt a similar attitude themselves.

This approach can be far from motivating and may paralyze rather than toughen the minds of human beings.

Despite all these, as observers, we are often expected to perceive them as fulfilled human beings. Questioning their attitude and not considering them close to a superhuman figure can sometimes lead to being labeled as envious of their remarkable tangible achievements or facing other similar labels.

Financial Education; Low-Hanging Fruit of Financial Success

Certainly, this book does not undermine the importance of the financial aspect of our lives or the value of financial education by any means. When our basic physical needs are not met, it is often impossible to explore any other dimensions of our being.

My own story serves as proof of how much I value the pursuit of financial freedom.

However, it is important to recognize that the concept of "financial freedom" can sometimes be misguiding and is often exploited by the trends of "Unisized Success" to foster a scarcity mindset for various reasons.

Financial freedom is a relative term and tied to our chosen lifestyle and personal preferences. Despite this obvious fact, it seems that financial freedom has been constantly used as an objective concept for marketing tactics.

It has been repeatedly mentioned in various course introductions, or relentlessly promoted in numerous seminars by individuals who make compelling promises of revealing the keys to achieving it.

If we take a moment to acknowledge that individuals have the freedom to choose their desired living standards from a wide range of options, the central focus shifts to their security and financial freedom within those chosen standards.

By promoting financial responsibility and educating people on how to develop better money habits, they can view financial freedom as a tangible goal based on their preferred lifestyle. They will not feel obligated to reach a specific financial level or status as a prerequisite for being considered financially free.

Nature-Type Abundance

Finding alternative sources of abundance that provide immediate rewards can help reduce the negative effects of a scarcity mindset imposed by such trends, especially for individuals with limited resources.

Nature stands out as one of the most important and easily accessible sources of abundance in our surroundings. The beauty and richness of nature are not exclusive to a select few; it is a free resource that everyone can access and enjoy regardless of their social status.

While not everyone can afford to own a luxurious house in a stunning resort, camping in the nearby area can also provide a unique sense of adventure and deep connection with nature that brings its own version of joy and satisfaction. Ultimately, one's perspective and mindset have an important role in determining the level of happiness derived from each experience.

For those who appreciate the captivating beauty of forests, every element carries a sense of awe: From the tiny insects to the mysterious sounds of nature, from the delightful experience of breathing in the fragrance of trees to physically embracing them and fully immersing ourselves in their remarkable generosity, as our lives literally depend on them.

The sky above us represents yet another source of abundance that symbolizes enormous possibilities, freedom, and limitless potential. Even in urban landscapes that may lack visual attractiveness, the sky always offers something valuable for those who take a moment to observe. The simple act of sky gazing can be a meditative practice that contributes to our calmness and inner peace in this hectic world.

When we were children, we all had a genuine fondness for nature. Youngsters show no concern about getting dirty while playing with soil; instead, they treat it as something magical.

Is it possible for us to reconnect with that inner child who once truly embraced the abundance of nature, or will such trends of success and greatness judge us as attempting to mask our insecurities and failures by seeking comfort in nature?

A real-life example of reclaiming one's inner child and pursuing their authentic dreams, rather than conforming to the trend of "Celebritized Greatness-Unisized Success," can be seen in Paola Merrill and her YouTube channel, TheCottageFairy.

Paola had the option to conform by pursuing a PhD, striving for a prestigious academic career, and she was on the path to attaining them. However, she made the courageous choice to follow "The Road Less Traveled."

Certainly, by "The Road Less Traveled," I am not referring to the current popular usage of this term on social media to emphasize the sacrifices required for achieving a high level of "Unisized Success."

While that definition can be meaningful within its specific context, what I intend to convey here is that Paola chose a path that aligned with her preferred version of success and greatness, and she is living her own dreams.

Despite facing some criticism and being labeled as someone who prioritizes a carefree life over advancing her career, Paola's genuine happiness, joy, and her special bond with nature serve as clear indications that she is truly living her own dreams, rather than someone else's.

A dream that cannot be traded or replaced is THE DREAM that is worth living our one and only life for...

www.ingramcontent.com/pod-product-compliance
Lightning Source LLC
LaVergne TN
LVHW090531110826
845146LV00003B/1055